The Star Fruit

and other stories

Sally Prue

Illustrated by
Jamie Hogan
Carol Liddiment
David Dean

CONTENTS

OXFORD
UNIVERSITY PRESS

Dear Reader,

Here are four stories all from different continents of the world. Two are about brothers, two are about gods, and two are about magical animals.

They are all about how tempting fruit can be, especially when it belongs to someone else.

Happy reading!

Sally Prue

The Star Fruit Tree

A folk tale from Vietnam

Chapter 1

 Long ago, a rich man died and left his two sons his enormous fortune.

'Hurray!' shouted the elder son, jumping about with glee. 'Father's finally dropped dead and I'm rich at last! I shall buy everything I want and eat cakes all day!'

'Yes, and we'll be able to help poor people, too,' said the younger son.

But the elder son was very greedy. He didn't want to give money to the poor. In fact, he didn't even want to share the money with his brother, much.

So the elder son sneaked down to his father's house that night and put new locks on all the doors.

'Sorry,' he said, when his brother arrived the next morning. 'I'm afraid you're too late. This is my house, now.'

The younger son was very surprised.

'But Father said his fortune was to be shared between us,' he pointed out.

Now the elder son was greedy and disagreeable, but he knew his younger brother was right. Their father's property had to be shared between them.

'Of course we must share!' he said grandly. 'I never thought of doing anything else. So ... er ... I'll have the house and everything in it, including the treasure chest and the silver teapot, and you get ...'

He looked around for something he didn't want. He'd just decided he was going to have to give his brother the doormat, when he noticed the star fruit tree that grew by the front gate.

'... the star fruit tree!' he proclaimed. The tree bore lots of golden fruit, but they were quite sour, especially to someone who scoffed as many cakes as he did.

So that was how it turned out. The elder son lived in his father's house, stuffing his face – and the younger son lived with his wife and children in their hut. All the younger son could do was water the star fruit tree and look forward to the day when he could take the first ripe star fruit to market.

Chapter 2

At last the day came when the first of the star fruit grew ripe. The younger son got up eagerly the next morning to pick the fruit for market. But when he ran up to the tree with his basket he found a huge raven slurping up the last of the ripe fruit.

Well, the next morning the raven was there again, and again the day after that.

The poor younger son didn't know what to do, so that evening he sat on the knobbly ground under the tree and waited for the raven to return.

The younger son waited there all night. The only company he had was the sound of his brother chomping cakes.

At last, as the sun rose over the mountain like a shining halo, a huge black bird flapped noisily through the sky. It landed with a thud in the branches of the star fruit tree.

The younger son scrambled to his feet.

'Excuse me,' he said, bowing politely. 'But is there any chance you could find yourself something else for breakfast? Some nice worms, perhaps? Because that fruit is all the fortune I have in the world. If you eat it my wife and children will starve.'

The raven sniffed.

'Huh!' he said, with star fruit juice dripping from his beak. 'Well, in that case perhaps *you* should try eating some nice worms!'

The younger son scratched his head.

'I see your point,' he admitted. 'Oh dear, what can I do?'

The raven looked surprised, which wasn't easy without eyebrows.

'Well, how about shooting me with an arrow?' he suggested. 'Or sticking me to the tree branches with invisible glue, and then putting me in a pie? That's what most people want to do.'

'Oh no,' said the younger son, horrified. 'I'd never dream of doing anything like that!'

The raven's eyes glittered down through the leaves of the star fruit tree.

'Well, in that case I suppose I'll have to pay you for the star fruit,' he said. 'Go and make yourself a bag with each side as long as the distance from the tip of your nose to your belly button, and come back here tomorrow.'

Chapter 3

The younger son hurried home. He told his wife what had happened and together they made a bag with sides as long as the distance from the tip of his nose to his belly button.

The next morning, sure enough, the raven landed in the star fruit tree with a great flopping and flapping of wings. He gobbled down all the ripe star fruit and then jumped down to the ground.

'Now climb up onto my back, my friend,' he said to the younger son. 'And I'll take you for a ride.'

So the younger son climbed onto the great bird's feathery, black back. The raven began flapping his wings like mad. Soon the star fruit tree and the younger son's hut were far below them.

The younger son was brave, as well as kind, but all the flapping made him dizzy. He had to keep his eyes tight shut to stop himself falling off. He had no idea where they were going until the raven landed so suddenly that the younger son bounced off the raven's back, rolled head over heels, and ended up on a pile of something that went *chink! chonk!* as he landed on it.

The younger son lay still for a moment and
wondered if he was dead.

Then he sat himself up, opened his eyes
and gasped with amazement.

He was surrounded by piles and piles of
shining, glistening gold coins. He picked
up a handful and let them fall twinkling
and chiming back onto the others.

'*Cor!*' he said.

'You sound like one of those silly crows,' the raven snorted. 'Now fill up your bag. We won't get back in time for breakfast if we don't hurry!'

So the younger son filled up his bag, then he climbed back onto the raven and closed his eyes.

Chapter 4

As soon as they landed back at the star fruit tree, the younger son thanked the raven and ran home carrying his heavy bag of gold.

His family were very happy. The younger son gave lots of money to the poor, and then he built a huge extension onto his hut which turned it into something that was almost a palace.

When the house was finally finished, he invited his elder brother to tea.

'Eat in your old hut?' said the elder son, scornfully.

'We've made a feast,' the younger son told him.

The elder son began to look interested.

'Any cakes?' he asked.

'More than anyone could eat,' said the younger son.

'Huh,' said the elder son. 'We'll see about that.'

And he put on his hat.

The elder son could hardly believe his eyes
when he saw the younger son's house.

And when the younger son told him about
the raven, he could hardly believe his ears.

'Oh my dear little brother,' cried the elder
son. 'You are so good and kind that you've
made me ashamed. If you want to make me
happy, please take all Father's fortune, and I'll
just have the star fruit tree.'

Well, the younger son was very glad his brother had become so generous, so he agreed at once.

The elder son immediately rushed back to the star fruit tree and waited until the raven arrived and started eating.

'Thief!' shouted the elder son. 'Pay for that fruit or I'll shoot you!'

'Oh all right,' said the raven, wearily. 'Tomorrow bring a bag with sides as long as the distance between the tip of your nose and your belly button.'

But the elder son made the biggest bag
he possibly could with some bed sheets.

'Off we go then,' said the raven, the
next morning.

The elder son was as wobbly as jelly by the
time he got to the mountain of gold, but he
filled up his enormous bag, and his pockets,
and even put a couple of coins in his mouth.

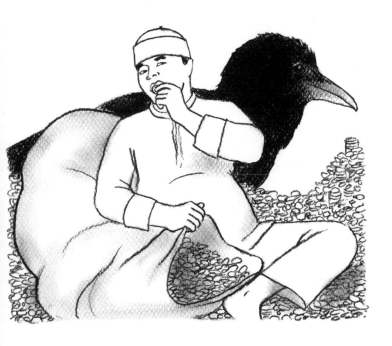

Then he climbed onto the raven's back.

But the raven was already tired from carrying the greedy brother all the way there, and of course all the gold was terribly heavy. By the time the raven flew over the sea, he was exhausted. His wings sagged and his head went down ...

... and suddenly the gold bag slipped off the raven's back.

The elder son grabbed it, but the gold was even heavier than he was and it dragged him down, down, into the murky depths of the sea. Where, as far as anyone knows, he still is.

The raven felt much better then. He soared upwards and flew back to the star fruit tree and helped himself to breakfast.

The younger son sometimes wondered what had happened to his brother. But, being the sort of person who never thought ill of anyone, he never guessed, and the raven never told him.

And so the younger son and his family lived happily ever after.

Big Snake's Gift

A myth from the Tupi tribes of the Amazon, in South America

Chapter 1

The world, when it was first made, was a strange place. For one thing the only animal was Big Snake, and for another it never got dark.

Now, that might sound quite fun. No night-time means no bedtime. It means no nightmares. It means no tripping over logs in the dark and hurting yourself.

But after a while, the endless day began to annoy people. The young man who was married to Big Snake's beautiful daughter was the most annoyed of all.

'Come on,' he was always saying to Big Snake's daughter, yawning until his ears ached. 'It *must* be time to go to bed.'

But Big Snake's daughter would look up at the bright sun that lit up the jungle leaves like lanterns.

'Oh no, it can't be time for bed yet,' she'd say. 'It's still light.'

Then the young man, who was only awake because he'd propped his eyelids open with little sticks, would groan. The groan was a long, sad noise like a jaguar with stomach ache. Of course, he didn't *know* it was like a jaguar with stomach ache because jaguars hadn't been invented yet, any more than the night-time had.

'I *know* it's light!' he'd say crossly. 'It's *always* light. The sun stays up all the time, and you carry on singing happily all the time. But as for me, *I need to get some sleep*!'

But the daughter of Big Snake only shrugged.

'You'll have to wake up the night, then,' she said. 'Then perhaps I'd feel like going to bed.'

The young man sighed. The night was still asleep under the waters of the great river. He knew he'd never be able to swim down far enough to find it. He sighed so sadly that Big Snake's daughter felt sorry for him.

'You should send someone to Big Snake,' she told him. 'He'll give you a spell to wake up the night, I'm sure.'

Now, the young man had three servants who were very clever at doing all sorts of things like making porridge, juggling and fetching things. So he sent them to Big Snake's house to get a magic spell to wake up the night.

Chapter 2

The three servants paddled their canoe along
the great river. Their hearts were heavy. Big
Snake was big, and he was a snake. The only
servant who wasn't completely terrified was the
smallest one, Knee-high. He reckoned that if
Big Snake was hungry, he would choose to eat
one of the bigger ones.

Big Snake's house was hung all round with
slimy creepers. Inside the house something was
hissing fiercely.

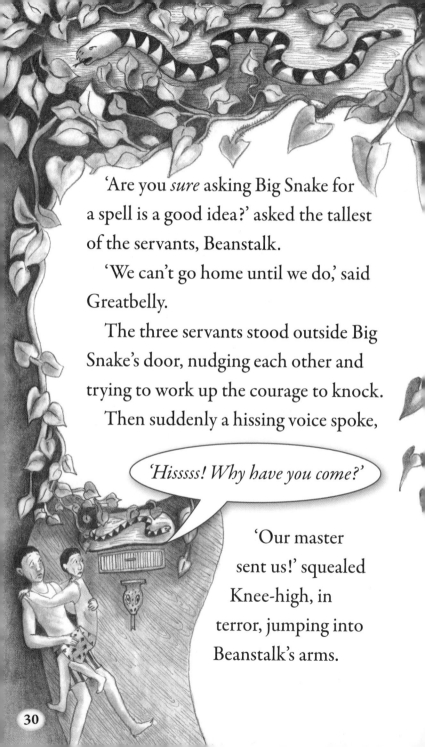

'Are you *sure* asking Big Snake for a spell is a good idea?' asked the tallest of the servants, Beanstalk.

'We can't go home until we do,' said Greatbelly.

The three servants stood outside Big Snake's door, nudging each other and trying to work up the courage to knock.

Then suddenly a hissing voice spoke,

'Hissss! Why have you come?'

'Our master sent us!' squealed Knee-high, in terror, jumping into Beanstalk's arms.

'To get a spell!' yelped Greatbelly, trying to hide behind the others.

'To wake up the night!' quavered Beanstalk.

There was a long pause. The only noise was a small chattering sound, which was being made by Knee-high's teeth.

Then the door of Big Snake's house opened a little. Something rolled out and came to rest at the servants' feet.

Greatbelly picked it up. It was a tucuma fruit.
'*There isss the ssspell*,' said the hissing voice.
'*Take it home, but do not open it. It isss very
powerful magic. If it isss opened too sssoon,
many thingsss that live in the world will be
changed forever.*'

Well, it didn't *look* like a spell – it looked like a tucuma fruit – but the three servants didn't hang about arguing. They jumped into their canoe and didn't stop paddling until they were a long way away from Big Snake's house.

Chapter 3

'Who is making that silly noise?' asked Knee-high, pausing in his paddling.

'The one that sounds like *ten, ten, len, zi*?' asked Beanstalk.

'That's right,' said Knee-high. 'One of those annoying noises that gets right inside your ears so you can't think about anything else. Who's making it?'

'Beanstalk,' said Greatbelly.

'Greatbelly,' said Beanstalk, at the same time.

They all stopped paddling and listened carefully.

Ten, ten, len, zi!

'*I think* ...' began Knee-high.

'... it's coming from inside the tucuma fruit!'
finished Beanstalk, picking it up and putting it
to one of his big ears.

Ten, ten, len, zi!

'Perhaps we should open the fruit and see
what's causing it,' suggested Greatbelly. 'It
might be something that's spoiling the spell.'

But Beanstalk put the tucuma fruit down
and started paddling again. Big Snake had told
them not to open the tucuma fruit, and Big
Snake was full of powerful magic.

The three servants paddled along the gleaming river for a long time. The tucuma fruit kept making little noises.

Ten, ten, len zi!

Suddenly Knee-high put down his paddle.

'That thing's driving me mad!' he exclaimed. 'I can't paddle another stroke until I know what's inside it.'

The others looked at each other.

'Perhaps we could just make a tiny, *tiny* hole,' suggested Beanstalk.

Greatbelly picked up the tucuma fruit and peered at it.

'It's only stuck together with tree sap,' he said. 'We can easily seal it up again afterwards.'

So the three servants paddled to the bank of the river and lit a fire. They held the tucuma fruit over the fire until the sap began to melt. Then it was easy to open the husk a little bit.

'Oh, look!' began Greatbelly. 'Look at that! I can see ...'

Suddenly, everything went completely dark.

'Oh *no*!' howled Beanstalk. 'Look what you've done!'

'I *can't* look, you idiot!' snapped Knee-high. 'It's gone all dark!'

'The night's woken up!' wailed Greatbelly. 'Our master will know we've opened the tucuma fruit, now!'

But neither Big Snake's daughter nor her husband were thinking about the three servants. As soon as night was released upon the earth, Big Snake's daughter yawned and decided it was time to go to bed.

As she and her husband slept, the world began to change, just as Big Snake had said it would. Many things were changed into birds and mammals and fish. A basket became a jaguar, and a fisherman in a canoe sprouted a beak and turned into a duck.

After many hours of darkness Big Snake's daughter woke up.

'I think it must be time to get up, now,' she said.

She took some string, dyed it with juice from the urucum fruit, and made it into a red-feathered cujubim bird. 'You, little bird, shall sing every morning to tell the sun when it's time to get up,' she said.

Then she took another string and made an inambu bird. 'You shall start singing at nightfall,' she told the bird.

In that way the daughter of Big Snake taught the birds to wake up the day and the night. And this they still do.

Chapter 4

A short while later, there was the sound of scurrying feet, and there, looking foolish, were Knee-high, Beanstalk and Greatbelly.

Their master frowned at them.

'So it was you who opened the tucuma fruit and made so many things turn into animals,' he said, sternly.

Knee-high shook his head and pointed accusingly at Beanstalk. But Beanstalk was already pointing at Greatbelly, who was pointing at Knee-high.

Big Snake's daughter shook her head.

'I think you must all have done it together,' she said. 'The sap that was sealing the tucuma fruit has melted over you. See, you have yellow stripes running down your arms.'

At that Greatbelly, Beanstalk and Knee-high jumped backwards guiltily. In fact, they jumped back so far they landed in the branches of a tree on the edge of the jungle.

Their master looked up at them.

'The world has changed because of what you did,' he said. 'You opened Big Snake's spell in the wrong way. Because of this, some things which should have stayed as they were have been changed into animals. I'm afraid you won't be able to be my servants any more.'

Greatbelly, Knee-high and Beanstalk howled at that. They jumped up and down with dismay.

Then they turned and swung themselves away through the jungle, hooting and howling at the tops of their voices.

As monkeys do.

The Mouth of the Baobab Tree

A myth from Africa

 **Long ago, when** the world was new, all the land was one big desert.

It was very beautiful, but sometimes the sand got too hot to sit on.

So the gods made some plants. They put these plants in holes and watered them, and the land began to turn green.

But it took millions of plants to cover even one valley, and the gods soon got backache.

• *baobab:* (say) 'bay-oh-bab'.   **45**

So they decided to make a big plant which would cover lots of ground in one go. They made it with a fat tall trunk and big leafy branches.

They called the plant a baobab tree.

Now, for a while the baobab tree was the tallest and fattest plant in the world. Animals made their homes in her trunk, or sheltered under her branches, and the baobab tree was extremely pleased with herself.

But then one day she looked out across the valley and saw something new.

'What's that scrawny thing over there?' she asked a passing camel.

'It's a new sort of tree, of course,' the camel said, down its nose. 'A fern tree.'

Well, the baobab tree peered over at the new fern tree. The fern tree was quite thin and weedy, but it was actually taller than she was.

'*Oi!*' she shouted, indignantly, rustling her leaves. Several gazelles turned their beautiful heads, but the baobab tree ignored them. '*Oi!*' she shouted again. 'You lot! Gods! You've made me all wrong, you have! I'm supposed to be the greatest tree in the world, and now you've made that silly fern tree taller than I am!'

Well, the gods were busy making some extra-long eyelashes for the ostrich, so they didn't have time to argue. They made the baobab tree a bit taller, and peace came back to the world.

But the next morning the baobab tree looked across the valley again. By the river she saw something bright and glowing.

'That's a flame tree,' explained an eagle, as he flew over. 'It's covered in flowers.'

The baobab tree was very angry.

'Is it, indeed!' she muttered. '*Oi!*' she bellowed. 'Gods! You've messed up again! I'm supposed to be the greatest tree in the world, but you haven't given me any flowers! *Oi!*'

Well, the gods were busy running after the cheetah to paint on his spots, so they quickly gave the baobab tree lots of beautiful flowers, and hoped she'd be quiet.

And she was quiet – until the next morning, when she spotted something growing at the bottom of the cliff.

'It's a fig tree,' the monkey told her, his mouth dripping with juice. 'Mmm, its fruit are absolutely delicious!'

Well, the baobab tree was *furious*.

'*Oi!*' she shouted across the plain, to where the gods were carving teeth for the crocodile. 'What sort of idiots are you? I should be growing *fruit*!'

The gods sighed. It's tricky making teeth, and even more difficult putting them into a crocodile's mouth. One of the more patient gods quickly made a fruit spell for the baobab tree, but the other gods were fed up.

'That tree makes a lot of noise,' said one.

'And she's very ungrateful,' said another.

'You know, I think we'd be better off if she was quieter,' said a third.

The gods looked at each other thoughtfully. Then they nodded.

First they made a spell which lifted the great baobab tree right up into the air ...

... and then they made a spell which turned her upside down ...

... and *then* they planted her like that, with her mouth in the earth and her roots in the air.

And that is how every baobab tree in the world has remained until this very day.

The Fruit Thief's Dance

(*A folk tale from New Zealand*)

Chapter 1

One day, two warriors were walking past a village when they saw a poporo tree laden with delicious fruit.

Now, Uenuku was the Chief of that village and he killed anyone he found stealing his fruit. The warriors needed to be cunning.

That evening the warriors, who were brothers called Tama and Rewi, made a pair of stilts. When it was dark, they crept quietly back to the outskirts of the village.

• *poporo:* (say) 'paw-paw-raw'. • *Uenuku:* (say) 'ooh-eh-noo-ku'.
• *Tama:* (say) 'tah-ma'. • *Rewi:* (say) 'reh-we'.

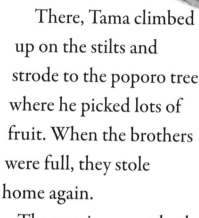

There, Tama climbed up on the stilts and strode to the poporo tree where he picked lots of fruit. When the brothers were full, they stole home again.

The warriors went back to the poporo tree night after night. It wasn't until they'd eaten nearly all the fruit that Chief Uenuku began to wonder what was happening.

The people of the village searched the ground for tracks. All they found were the marks of Tama's stilts.

Chapter 2

The next night the villagers hid inside Uenuku's house. As soon as they heard the thumping of Tama's stilts coming along, the villagers jumped out. They caught Rewi at the edge of the village, but Tama escaped on his high stilts. The villagers didn't catch up with him until he'd reached the beach.

'Chop down his stilts!' ordered Chief Uenuku.

'No, no, I might hurt myself!' cried Tama the warrior. 'Let me wade into the sea, first, so I fall on something soft!'

But of course the villagers chopped down his stilts straight away, and Tama came down onto the beach with a great *crash*! He picked himself up, however, and dodging like a bird escaped from a trap, he managed to get away.

Chief Uenuku was furious at Tama's escape. He stormed back to the village meaning to kill Rewi at once. But just as he was about to chop off Rewi's head, one of the villagers spoke up:

'Chief, why should the fruit thief die so easily? If we took him into your house and hung him over the fire, that would smoke him like a fish.'

Well, Uenuku thought that was a brilliant idea. They hung up Rewi from the roof of Uenuku's house, and that night Uenuku invited everyone to a big party with lots of music and dancing.

In the forest Tama heard the noise of the party and was very sad. When the music died down Tama crept into the dark village and climbed up the thatched roof of Uenuku's house. He soon found a small hole.

'It's me, Tama,' he whispered. 'Are you dead, Rewi?'

'Not yet,' whispered Rewi. 'But I almost wish I were. Uenuku is going to hold a party every night while I'm dying. And the music in this village is so awful that even the lizards put their hands over their ears.'

Tama thought hard.

'Tomorrow, when the music starts, make a real fuss,' he told his brother. 'Tell the villagers they dance like turtles. And then, when they ask if you could do any better, say you could.'

So that was exactly what Rewi did.

At first the villagers scoffed.

'You can't dance!' they said.

'Oh yes I can,' boasted Rewi. 'I'm famous. My dancing's much better than the out-of-date stuff you do.'

'All right,' said the villagers, untying him. 'Show us.'

'With ash all over me?' asked Rewi. 'You must be joking. I'll have to wash,' he went on. 'And then I'll need something smart to wear. Oh, and I need a two-handed sword to dance with, as well.'

So the villagers gave him water, and the chief's red apron, and a two-handed sword. Then Rewi jumped into the firelight, ready to dance.

Well, Rewi stuck out his tongue, made hideous faces and punched and kicked the air. That was reckoned very fine dancing in those days. He danced all the way to the doorway. By then he was sweating.

'Open the door a bit,' he said. 'When I've cooled down I'll sing you a brilliant new song.'

There were so many villagers that there was no chance of Rewi out-running them all. So one of the villagers opened the door.

But as soon as the door was open Rewi leapt backwards right out of the house. Then before the villagers knew what was happening Tama jumped out of his hiding place. He slammed the door shut again and bolted it with two large sticks.

There was nothing the villagers inside Uenuku's house could do then, except shout for help.

By the time someone let them out, Rewi and Tama were miles away, eating poporo fruit as they went.